Author/ Publisher C.A. Sallenger
U.S.A.

Illustrated by: C.A. Sallenger

References:
Encyclopedia Smithsonian: Butterflies
Answers.com
Ask.com

Butterfly in the Wind Poem:
(wishuponabutterfly.com)

Other Books by C.A. Sallenger

Kindle e-books :

Where Do Clouds Come From?
(filled with facts, photos, and a cloud quiz.)

The History of the Saddle
(filled with facts and full color illustrations.)

Stories
(a collection of short stories for kids.)

Butterfly in the Wind Poem

A child is .....
A butterfly in the wind.
Some can fly higher than others,
but each one flies the best it can.
Each one is different!
Each one is special!
Each one is beautiful!

Author
unknown...

Butterflies belong to an order of insects called 'Lepidoptera' [lep-i-dop-ter-uh].

There are believed to be between 15,000 and 25,000 species of butterflies in the world.

Butterflies can be found everywhere in the world except Antarctica. It is to cold there and they do not have a food source.

Butterflies are cold blooded and enjoy the warmth of the sun.

The average lifespan of a butterfly is about two weeks depending on the species. Some species live for only a few days while others may live for several months.

Butterflies go through a process called 'Metamorphosis' [met-a-mor-pho-sis] or a drastic change.

A female butterfly lays tiny eggs on a leaf. Each egg contains a tiny caterpillar. Within a few days the tiny caterpillars are ready to hatch. Each caterpillar chews a hole in one end of it's egg and crawls out.

The caterpillars eat leaves. A lot of leaves as they grow bigger.

Monarch Butterfly egg

(shown larger than actual size)

Monarch Caterpillar

As the caterpillar grows it sheds it's skin several times. When the caterpillar begins to shed it's skin one last time, it hangs from the underside of a branch. While hanging under the branch the caterpillar forms a kind of cocoon around itself. This cocoon is called a pupa or chrysalis. The caterpillar will hang inside this chrysalis for about a week and a half.

While the caterpillar is hanging inside the chrysalis a great transformation takes place.

At the end of the week and a half the caterpillar emerges from the chrysalis as a butterfly.

Monarch Chrysalis

Monarch Butterfly emerging from chrysalis

Monarch Butterfly

Swallowtail Butterfly

Red Spotted Purple Butterfly

Pallas's Fritillary Butterfly

Peleides Blue Morpho Butterfly

Red Admiral
Butterfly

Blue Morpho
Butterfly

Common Blue
Butterfly

Tiger Swallowtail
Butterfly

Common Mormon Butterfly

Peacock Butterfly

Glasswing Butterfly

Quiz
And
Coloring book

1. Butterflies lay eggs on...

   a) the ground

   b) tree trunks

   c) leaves

2. Butterflies go through a process called...

   a) Lepidoptera

   b) metamorphosis

   c) chrysalis

3. Butterflies belong to an order of insects called...

   a) pupa

   b) Lepidoptera

   c) transformers

4. How long does it take for a caterpillar to become a butterfly?

   a) 1 month

   b) 5 weeks

   c) 1 1/2 weeks

5. Butterflies live in Antarctica.

   a) true

   b) false

6. There are only 1,000 species of butterflies in the world.

   a) true

   b) false

7. Butterflies are cold blooded.

   a) true

   b) false

8. The average lifespan of a butterfly is about 2 weeks.

   a) true

   b) false

9. Butterfly eggs contain tiny caterpillars.

   a) true

   b) false

10. The caterpillars shed their skin several times.

   a) true

   b) false

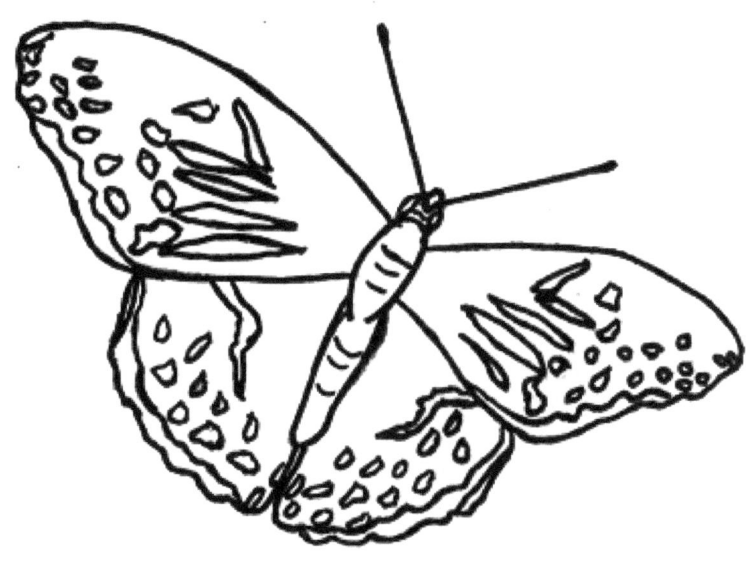

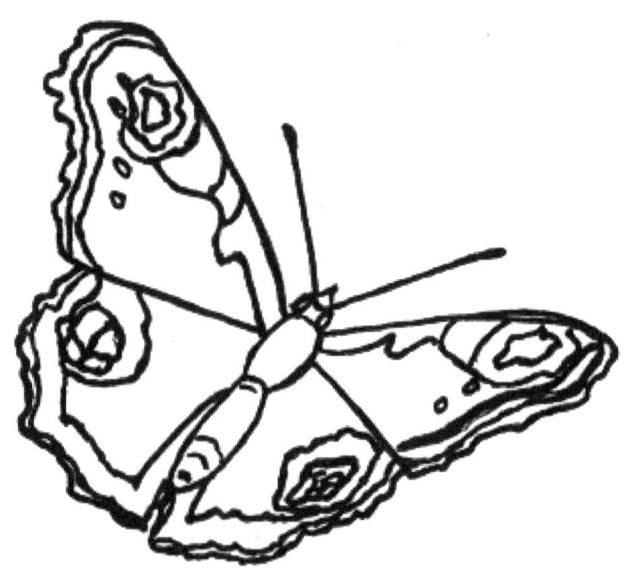

Quiz answers

1. C / leaves

2. B / metamorphosis

3. B / Lepidoptera

4. C / 1 1/2 weeks

5. B / false

6. B / false

7. A / true

8. A / true

9. A / true

10. A / true

www.ingramcontent.com/pod-product-compliance
Lightning Source LLC
Chambersburg PA
CBHW040316010626
45792CB00022B/588